IT'S TIME TO EAT LONGANS

It's Time to Eat LONGANS

Walter the Educator

Silent King Books
A WhichHead Entertainment Imprint

Copyright © 2024 by Walter the Educator

All rights reserved. No part of this book may be reproduced in any manner whatsoever without written per- mission except in the case of brief quotations embodied in critical articles and reviews.

First Printing, 2024

Disclaimer

This book is a literary work; the story is not about specific persons, locations, situations, and/or circumstances unless mentioned in a historical context. Any resemblance to real persons, locations, situations, and/or circumstances is coincidental. This book is for entertainment and informational purposes only. The author and publisher offer this information without warranties expressed or implied. No matter the grounds, neither the author nor the publisher will be accountable for any losses, injuries, or other damages caused by the reader's use of this book. The use of this book acknowledges an understanding and acceptance of this disclaimer.

It's Time to Eat LONGANS is a collectible early learning book by Walter the Educator suitable for all ages belonging to Walter the Educator's Time to Eat Book Series. Collect more books at WaltertheEducator.com

USE THE EXTRA SPACE TO TAKE NOTES AND DOCUMENT YOUR MEMORIES

LONGANS

It's time to eat, come gather near,

It's Time to Eat

Longans

A special treat is waiting here.

Round and small with a golden glow,

A fruit called longan, let's say hello!

The skin is thin, so gently peel,

A treasure hides, oh what a deal!

Inside it's juicy, sweet, and white,

A tasty snack, pure delight!

Like little gems from nature's tree,

Longan fruit is fun, you'll see.

Pop it in and take a bite,

It's soft and chewy, what a sight!

The seed inside is dark as night,

But don't you eat it, just hold it tight.

Set it aside, then grab some more,

Longan fruit's a tasty score!

It's Time to Eat
Longans

From lands where sunshine loves to play,

This fruit will brighten any day.

It's healthy too, so let's all cheer,

For longan fruit, a treat sincere!

Peel, then taste, and share with friends,

The fun with longan never ends.

Its sweetness spreads like joy so true,

A bite of love for me and you!

Let's thank the tree, so tall and kind,

For growing treats that we can find.

Nature's gift, so fresh and neat,

Longan fruit is hard to beat!

Enjoy each bite, so soft and sweet,

A snack so simple, such a treat.

Longan fruit, so small and round,

It's Time to Eat
Longans

The yummiest joy that can be found!

So next time when it's snack time fun,

Reach for longan, one by one.

A little fruit that's big on cheer,

Let's eat it up, it's finally here!

Now let's all munch, our bellies sing,

For longan fruit is the snack-time king.

Thank you, longan, sweet and round,

It's Time to Eat Longans

The best of treats that we have found!

ABOUT THE CREATOR

Walter the Educator is one of the pseudonyms for Walter Anderson. Formally educated in Chemistry, Business, and Education, he is an educator, an author, a diverse entrepreneur, and he is the son of a disabled war veteran. "Walter the Educator" shares his time between educating and creating. He holds interests and owns several creative projects that entertain, enlighten, enhance, and educate, hoping to inspire and motivate you. Follow, find new works, and stay up to date with Walter the Educator™ at WaltertheEducator.com

www.ingramcontent.com/pod-product-compliance
Lightning Source LLC
LaVergne TN
LVHW052013060526
838201LV00059B/4006